ACRL ACTIVE GUIDE

Designing Training

Melanie Hawks

Association of College and Research Libraries
A Division of the American Library Association
Chicago 2013

ACRL ACTIVE GUIDES

Active Guides is an occasional series published by ACRL. They provide a focused exploration of a given topic. Each guide highlights a workplace issue facing library professionals and offers both a theoretical perspective and several practical applications. The theoretical perspective examines an approach, model, or specific tool related to the issue and will lay the groundwork for the applications.

Other guidebooks currently available include:

Life-Work Balance
Conversations that Work
Influencing without Authority
Pay it Forward: Mentoring New Information Professionals

Library of Congress Cataloging-in-Publication Data

Hawks, Melanie.
  Designing training / by Melanie Hawks.
     pages cm. -- (ACRL active guide ; 5)
  Includes bibliographical references and index.
  ISBN 978-0-8389-8671-4 (pbk. : alk. paper) 1. Library employees--In-service training. 2. Library education (Continuing education) 3. Library institutes and workshops--Planning. 4. University of Utah. Libraries--Case studies. 5. Employees--Training of. 6. Training. I. Title.
  Z668.5.H39 2013
  023'.8--dc23
                    2013028744

Printed in the United States of America.

17 16 15 14 13   5 4 3 2 1

TABLE OF CONTENTS

INTRODUCTION

Think of the best teacher you ever had in school—the one you learned the most from. What made this person so effective? Was it the textbook and lesson plans she used? Or the test questions he wrote? Chances are, you don't even remember the textbooks, lesson plans, and test questions. You probably do remember the way she helped you overcome your frustration with a tricky math concept or the way he helped you fall in love with Renaissance art. Great teachers don't just instruct us; they change something within us.

Your aspirations as a trainer may be more modest in scope. Maybe you are less interested in being remembered as a "great teacher" than you are in surviving a major software rollout or getting a new batch of student employees up to speed on your policies. No matter how grand or humble your goals, keep in mind that all learning is ultimately about change. When we learn, we move along a continuum from ignorance to awareness, confusion to understanding, clumsiness to competence, apathy to caring. Even the most desirable change is hard. The goal of this book is to help you figure out what kind of change you're hoping to make in your learners and how to make that process easier them and for you.

How Trainers Add Value

A few years ago, I had the unpleasant experience of observing another trainer present a workshop that, as it turned out, he knew very little about. His training consisted mainly of reading aloud from the workbook participants had been given. When they asked questions, he stumbled over answering and quickly moved on to the next topic. He was obviously unfamiliar with the content he was presenting. In my opinion, that workshop was a waste of everyone's time; participants could have gotten the same information by simply reading the workbook themselves, and we

5

all could have avoided the awkwardness of watching someone flail around out of his depth.

Since then, I've challenged myself and others to consider the real value of a proposed training program or session: how will this training be any different, or better, than what participants could get from simply reading a manual (or reading a book, watching an online tutorial, etc)? How will the trainer add value beyond just presenting content?

I've come to believe that trainers add the most value through the design process. Effective delivery is also important, as demonstrated by my example above. But a well-designed training is one that sets up both the trainer and the learners to succeed. A well-designed training will enable the trainer to move learners toward specific learning goals.

How to Use This Guide

I've divided this guide into four sections that address what I believe are the four key elements of effective training design. Each section contains examples from my own practice and activities you can incorporate into yours. Reflections will prompt you to think critically about the guide's content and the examples I provide. Activities are meant to lead you through the design process for a single, specific training session that you are responsible for creating. If you don't have a real example to use right now, you can "redesign" a something you've previously created as a trainer or participated in as a learner. You may want to read through a section completely before going back to do the Activities.

- Section 1. Designing for the Adult Learner
  This section will help you understand who your learners are and what they need from your training session.

- Section 2. Designing for Takeaway Value
  This section will help you identify the purpose and scope of your training and communicate expectations to learners.

- Section 3. Designing for Purposeful Engagement
  This section will help you decide how to structure your training so that it is closely aligned with learning outcomes.

- Section 4: Designing for Learning Transfer
  This section will help you prepare learners for applying new concepts and skills in the real world.

A Note on Appendices

I've included four appendices that illustrate how I've applied the principles in this book to my own training. In 2010, my library implemented a new OPAC, Primo. I co-designed a staff training program intended to take us through the initial stages of implementation. The goal of this stage of training was mainly familiarization—ensuring that everyone could use the basic features of the new system by the time we went live. I will refer to the appendices throughout the book so that you can see an example of the product of the design process. These documents are included with grateful acknowledgement to my co-designer, Kate Holvoet, Associate Professor and Learning Commons Supervisor, Zayed University (Abu Dhabi and Dubai).

I've also included an appendix that summarizes a variety of options available when it's time to decide how you want to deliver your training. That material is based on 20 years of practice in the field, and is therefore meant to be more descriptive (what I've learned from experience) than prescriptive.

ACTIVITY

Briefly describe the real-life example you will use for the activities in this guide.

_____

_____

_____

_____

_____

_____

_____

_____

_____

_____

_____

_____

_____

_____

_____

_____

_____

_____

SECTION 1:
DESIGNING FOR THE ADULT LEARNER

Focus on the Learner

Your best teacher was great because she wasn't just thinking about how to get through the material. He wasn't just thinking about dates, places, and ideas. She was thinking about *you*—what you knew and didn't know, how you felt, and what you needed. He was thinking about the kind of person he wanted you to become.

Many teachers and trainers make the mistake of focusing too much on their subject matter and conveying information. Content is important, but it is a means, not an end. Would you rather ride in a car with someone who has memorized a driver's manual or someone who has driven for 20 years without an accident?

Some teachers and trainers focus on themselves, attempting to "perform" for an audience. While most learners would prefer to be taught by someone who is engaging, dynamic, and confident, they don't simply want an expert or an entertainer. They want someone who talks *with* them, not *to* them.

Your effectiveness will depend in large part on how well you connect with learners. This in turn will depend on how much you have thought about who your learners are and who you want to help them become.

Understand Where the Learner Is

If the whole point of learning is to change, an effective teacher or trainer must have some sense of where the learner currently is. Your best teacher didn't ask you to read *Don Quixote* in Spanish on the first day of class or

9

run a 6-minute mile without training. Instead, she probably started you with simple Spanish vocabulary and phrases or timed you to see how fast your mile was.

In *Telling Ain't Training*, Harold Stolovitz identifies three major factors that can help you determine a learner's starting point: ability, prior knowledge, and motivation.

Ability is based on a learner's talent for a particular type of activity. In *Now, Discover Your Strengths*, Marcus Buckingham and Daniel Clifton define talents as "naturally recurring patterns of thought, feeling, or behavior." A person's potential for learning can be enhanced or inhibited by his or her talents. I have no artistic talent; I struggle to create even the most simplistic line drawings during a game of Pictionary. I therefore struggled in studio art classes all through school. No matter how much I wanted to learn, or how hard I tried, I just couldn't produce the level of work that some classmates could. On the other hand, I have always had a talent for language. I was an early reader and excelled in writing assignments. I learned spelling and vocabulary words without even trying.

Prior Knowledge describes the level of experience, education, or training the learner already possesses. I've used PowerPoint for more than 15 years, for all different types of presentations (formal, informal, text-based, visual-based, etc.). I experimented with it quite a bit in graduate school when I studied information design and visual communication as part of my professional communication program. I'm mostly self-taught, though I've read (or at least skimmed) some of the recent books that explain how PowerPoint and other presentation tools can be used to greatest effect.

Motivation stems from a combination of the learner's mood and confidence as well as the value he or she attaches to the subject matter. For years, I promised myself that I would learn to use Prezi, an online software program that lets users create highly visual presentations. I felt like it would help me break out of my PowerPoint rut and challenge me to rethink the way I connected with audiences. Every time I sat down to try it out, I ended up quitting after just a few minutes. The frustration I felt fumbling around with this new tool reminded me of a particularly stressful semester in grad school, during which I had somehow found myself in an intensive, hands-on InDesign course. I had never used a professional graphics or desktop publishing program before; my classmates were mostly advertising and marketing people who could have taught the course themselves. With that experience still fresh in my mind, learning Prezi didn't seem like the best use of my time: why invest hours just learning a new tool that I might not ever get the hang of when I could instead spend that same amount of time creating a complete presentation in a familiar tool like PowerPoint?

Reflection Questions

Imagine that you are responsible for training me to use Prezi. How would you describe me as a learner for this subject (in terms of ability, prior knowledge, and motivation)?

_____

_____

_____

How would understanding me as a learner influence the way you designed the training?

_____

_____

_____

_____

Account for Different Levels of Ability, Knowledge, and Motivation

When I worked for the Association of Research Libraries, I conducted management workshops for groups of up to 40 people who often came from several different institutions. You can imagine the different levels of ability, knowledge, and motivation around the room. Some of our participants claimed more than 20 years of management experience; others had never supervised anyone. Some were eager to spend several days reflecting, practicing, and engaging; others made it clear that they were attending under duress. I know this because we sent a "Confidential Inquiry" prior to each of our workshops. Here are the questions we asked:

- What is the nature of your current position responsibilities? (if you supervise others, please include the number and level of staff supervised.)
- What are your primary expectations of this institute?
- Please describe any current problem(s) associated with your position that you hope to address or resolve through attendance at this training institute.
- What other management or leadership training have you received?

The responses helped us assess our learners' ability, prior knowledge, and motivation, which in turn helped us to figure out where the group's "starting point" might be. For example, sometimes people would disclose that they were struggling with the interpersonal communication skills required in a management position, because they strongly preferred working with tasks and processes instead (*ability*). This cued us to reassure participants that there is no one best way to manage, that there are ways to compensate for our limitations, and that we would offer many practical skill-building opportunities to help them become better communicators. Sometimes we would find out that most participants had already attended another of our workshops previously (*prior knowledge*); this prompted us to include specific call-backs to concepts they were already familiar with. Other times, we would learn that several participants had no idea what the workshop was about or why they were being asked to attend (*motivation*). This told us that we would need to include an early opportunity for participants to identify their own learning goals, and later opportunities to chart progress toward those goals.

ACTIVITY

Design a "confidential inquiry" for your learners. What would you ask them that would help you to assess their ability, knowledge, and motivation?

If this type of document is not practical for your purposes, how could you get some of the same information?

_____

_____

_____

_____

_____

_____

_____

_____

_____

_____

More recently, I was faced with helping to design the training modules to familiarize all of our employees with the public interface of the library's new online catalog. My colleague and I quickly identified two different audiences for this training. One audience ("Basic Users") consisted of non-experts whose job functions didn't require them to use the catalog on a regular basis (administrative staff, digital scanning technicians, etc.). The other audience ("Patron Service") consisted of people who were expert users of the previous system and who would need to use the new one as a primary tool for their jobs (such as librarians and staff who worked at public desks). This group had a higher level of prior knowledge and, presumably, a higher level of motivation for learning the new system. You can see how we used this information to help us design the right kind of training for each group. Appendix 1 shows a planning document we created for the "Basic Users" group; Appendix 2 shows the planning document we used for the "Patron Service" group.

Reflection Question

How do the two planning documents account for different levels of knowledge and motivation in the two different audiences?

_____

_____

_____

_____

_____

_____

_____

_____

Using the Three Factors

Ability

Assessing ability is tricky because learners don't always recognize their strengths and weaknesses and you may not have access to more objective information. Given these limitations, one simple assessment technique involves simply asking learners to describe their abilities. The information you get may not be perfect, but it will at least give you some idea of how learners perceive themselves and how they compare to each other.

Examples

How easy/difficult is it for you to learn new technologies?

___ very easy
___ somewhat easy
___ moderately difficult
___ very difficult

Compared to your peers, how would you rate your ability to speak in public?

___ about the same as most
___ seems to be a little easier for me
___ seems to be a lot easier for me
___ seems to be a little harder for me
___ seems to be a lot harder for me

The last time we upgraded/changed our software program, how soon were you able to use the new version proficiently?

___ right away without any training
___ right away after the training
___ after some additional practice/help
___ after a lot of additional practice/help
___ I never quite got the hang of it

Prior Knowledge

On the surface, it seems as though prior knowledge is an advantage to learning. I've found that it's sometimes just the opposite. What people already know can inhibit learning—the more they know, the more they may have to change. I got frustrated trying to use Prezi because it was so different from PowerPoint. A few years ago, I co-authored a paper with a very experienced academic who kept inserting two spaces after every period (and "correcting" my single spaces) even after I explained that Chicago, MLA, and APA all call for a single space. At my library, people have a lot of prior experience with evacuating the building, thanks to previous construction projects and a recent cold, wet winter with bursting pipes. Changing our evacuation procedures would require people to forget what we have drilled into them for years. People sometimes need to "unlearn" quite a bit before they can adopt new ways of thinking or behaving. You can facilitate unlearning by attending to the change process. If we needed to train our library staff in a new evacuation procedure, we would need to:

Acknowledge the Change
"The old emergency procedure required us to assemble on the south side of the plaza after an evacuation. The new procedure requires us to assemble on the north side."

Paint a Picture of the Change
"Here is a campus map showing our old assembly point by the fountain, and our new assembly point by the campus bulletin board."

Be Explicit About New Behaviors
"This means that you'll go to your left when you exit the building instead of your right. Walk toward the Union building and look for the security staff person in an orange vest near the campus bulletin board."

Provide Practice Opportunities

"Next week we will hold an evacuation drill so you'll have a chance to get used to the new procedure."

Offer 'Point of Change' Help

"We will station our security staff right outside the doors to steer you to the new assembly point."

Motivation

Remember that a learner's motivation may be very different from your own and will be affected by a lot of issues outside your control. According to Harold Stolovitz, three factors influence adult learner motivation.

Need

One of the reasons I put off learning Prezi for so long was that my "old" way of doing things in PowerPoint worked just fine. In the absence of a demand for me to change, I stayed in my comfort zone. Adults are more motivated when they see a good reason to learn. I finally motivated myself to learn Prezi by setting a goal to use it for a specific presentation I had on my schedule; this created a need for me to learn, albeit an artificial one. Most training done in an organizational setting is driven by external factors: a new policy or procedure, an upgraded software version, an identified service delivery problem, and so forth. It is important to make sure your learners understand how the training connects to organizational goals and priorities and how it will help them perform their jobs better.

Choice

Late last year I was tasked with getting about 100 of my coworkers to attend a mandatory training. I knew this would be difficult, not just logistically, but motivationally. The topic of the training was obviously important—we don't often require participation from so many employees across the whole organization—but the more people feel like they're being forced to learn, the less open they are to learning. In order to give my coworkers a little bit of autonomy, I presented them with several options: they could attend one of two live, in-person training sessions, or watch a recorded version during one of two group viewings I set up, or watch the recording independently on our streaming server. All of these options removed the logistical barriers to participation people otherwise might have faced, but they also let people decide for themselves which format would best meet their needs. Wherever possible, give your learners some choice over what, when, and how to learn.

Application

When I worked for my university's campus training department, we offered a half-day "Leading Change" workshop. It had been designed by trainers who preceded our group. The first time I reviewed the material, I saw that it had been designed around John Kotter's change model. Kotter's model includes steps such as "Form a Powerful Coalition" and "Anchor the Changes in Corporate Culture"—in other words, it's a model that mainly speaks to an organization's top-level leadership, those who are responsible for formulating large-scale strategy. Most of the people attending our workshops were mid-level managers, team leaders, and unit supervisors. They were responsible for implementing change at the ground level; Kotter's model just wasn't something they could apply. I redesigned the workshop to focus on strategies and skills that were more relevant to our audience. Adults need to believe that they can use what they're learning—that they will have opportunities to apply new knowledge and skills. To increase learner motivation, make sure your content is matched to your participants. It should be relevant, practical, and actionable.

Know How You Want Learners to Change

There's no point in starting if you don't know where you're going. Your favorite teacher had a plan—you would recognize major works of art, conjugate a set of verbs, or understand what led to the Civil War by the end of the year.

How will learners be different as a result of your training? Learning objectives keep both the trainer and the learners focused on outcomes, not just topics. They give the training purpose and direction. They can also help you decide what's most important to cover if your time is limited. You can potentially guide learners to change three things: what they **know**, what they **do**, and how they **feel**.

Effective learning objectives describe how the learners' knowledge, skills, or attitudes will be different as a result of the training.

> **Knowledge**: facts; steps in a process; general concepts
> **Skills**: behaviors; abilities; applied knowledge
> **Attitudes**: beliefs; emotions; perceptions; values; judgments

If you've looked at Appendices 1 and 2, you've already seen a real-life example of learning objectives. We will revisit learning objectives in the next section, where you will have a chance to practice creating them.

The Experiential Learning Cycle

David Kolb's theory of adult learning suggests that people learn by engaging in a spiral process that usually begins with a concrete experience. In everyday life, this process often starts when we encounter a problem or an unfamiliar situation.

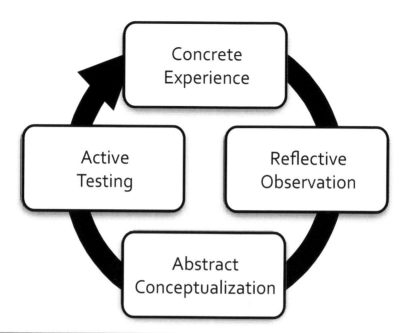

STAGE OF CYCLE	ACTIVITY	REAL-LIFE EXAMPLE
Concrete Experience	Something happens	No one has followed through on what we agreed were next steps on a project
Reflective Observation	Learner tries to make sense of what happened	We didn't document our agreement or set timelines; everyone is really busy and some people said they didn't know who was supposed to do what
Abstract Conceptualization	Learner draws insights & general conclusions based on his/her understanding of the experience	People need clear expectations and accountability; agreeing in principle doesn't always translate to action
Active Testing	Learner puts insights & conclusions into practice	At the next meeting, we will create a list of action items assigned to specific people and attached to deadlines

Kolb describes the process as a spiral because learning does not end with the completion of one cycle. A learner who is testing new ideas, approaches, and skills begins a new cycle; the test becomes another experience.

This process often happens outside of our conscious awareness; we don't think of ourselves as learning when we sit down to hash out what went wrong on a project team and what we should do to fix it. And sometimes, of course, we don't learn anything from an experience because we are too busy putting out fires, assigning blame, or rushing to the next appointment. In a training context, you can plan to lead learners through the experiential learning cycle with activities that prompt them to move from having an experience to deciding how to test new ideas/apply new information. One of the most common methods is known as **debriefing**. Debriefing consists of asking questions and facilitating discussion around an experience that learners have just had.

For instance, imagine that you are teaching a workshop on giving feedback. One of your activities is a role play where learners pair up and practice delivering feedback; this is the Concrete Experience stage. When the role play is over, you debrief by asking several questions for each subsequent stage.

Reflective Observation: What Happened?
- What happened when you gave your partner feedback?
- How did you feel about having to discuss sensitive topics?
- Did anything surprise you?
- Was this a comfortable experience for you? Uncomfortable?
- When you were receiving feedback, what did your partner say or do that you found helpful?
- Which parts of this process were easier for you? Which were more difficult?

Abstract Conceptualization: So What?

- Was this practice activity similar to or different from real feedback sessions you've had?
- What does this activity tell us about giving and receiving feedback?
- Based on this experience, what do you think are the most important principles of giving and receiving feedback?
- How would your relationships with people at work be different if everyone talked with each other this way?

Active Testing: Now What?

- How can you see yourself using this process in real life?
- Does any part of the process stand out as particularly useful to you?
- Where would you apply the tools we've worked with today?

SECTION 2:
DESIGNING FOR TAKEAWAY VALUE
Meaningful Learning Objectives

How will learners be different as a result of your training? Learning objectives keep both the trainer and the learners focused on outcomes, not just topics. They give the training purpose and direction. They can also help you decide what's most important to cover if your time is limited.

You can potentially guide learners to change three things: their **knowledge**, their **skills**, and their **attitudes**.

	KNOWLEDGE	SKILLS	ATTITUDES
Relates To:	facts; steps in a process; general concepts; theories	behaviors; abilities; applied knowledge	beliefs; emotions; values; judgments; perceptions
Example	Identify the major works of Edgar Allan Poe	Perform a dramatic interpretation of *The Tell-Tale Heart*	Appreciate Poe's contribution to the development of American literature
Key Words	understand; define; describe; identify	use; apply; demonstrate; analyze; assess; perform; decide	realize; understand why; recognize the value/ importance of; appreciate

Effective learning objectives describe how the learners' knowledge, skills, or attitudes will be different as a result of the training.

INEFFECTIVE OBJECTIVE	EFFECTIVE OBJECTIVE	WHAT WILL BE DIFFERENT?
Discuss learning objectives *This describes an activity you will engage in around a certain topic, but it doesn't describe how learners will be different as a result*	Understand what learning objectives are and how they fit into the design process	**Knowledge**: learners will know how objectives can be used to guide design
	Write learning objectives that focus on knowledge, skills, and attitudes	**Skill**: learners will be able to translate general knowledge about objectives into creating a specific product
	Recognize the importance of writing effective learning objectives	**Attitude**: learners will be more likely to actually write objectives if they believe in their importance

Depending on your subject matter and audience, you may emphasize some types of learning objectives more than others. Be careful not to overlook the benefits of attitudinal objectives even for what may seem like relatively straightforward skill-based trainings. For example, if you were training library staff in using EndNote, you might want to include an attitudinal objective such as "Appreciate the benefit of using EndNote to manage citations." This would ensure that you spent some time explaining why it's worth people's time to learn, and why your library is emphasizing EndNote over other similar products.

In the next section we'll talk about how to use your learning objectives to help you decide on the best way to deliver your content.

ACTIVITY

For each objective listed below, decide which type it best fits into; is it intended to change knowledge, skills, or attitudes? Explain why in the column on the far right.

OBJECTIVE	TYPE: KNOWLEDGE, SKILLS, OR ATTITUDES?	EXPLANATION
Recognize the value of engaging in difficult conversations		
Identify the barriers to engaging in difficult conversations		
Assess personal readiness to engage in dialogue		
Identify strategies for lowering defensiveness		
Decide whether to hold a difficult conversation		
Use a template to plan a difficult conversation		

ACTIVITY

Write at least three learning objectives for your training—one for each type (knowledge, skills, and attitudes).

Knowledge Objective:

_____

_____

_____

_____

_____

_____

Skills Objective:

_____

_____

_____

_____

_____

_____

Attitudes Objective:

_____

_____

_____

_____

_____

_____

Evaluating Learning

The beauty of learning objectives is that they simultaneously help you plan what to deliver on the front-end, and how to evaluate its effectiveness on the back-end. Learners should leave the session feeling that their time was well spent and feeling confident about their ability to perform in the real world. It's also important for trainers to know, as soon as possible, whether the training they designed served its intended purpose. Learning objectives can serve as your evaluation criteria. Appendix 3 shows how we did this with the learning objectives we developed for Primo. I had come up with the idea for the Training Outcomes Checklist earlier, when I wanted a simple way to assess learning relative to course objectives. Over time I found that the checklist lent itself well to technical training where learners could immediately self-assess. It didn't work so well for "soft skills" training (such as interpersonal communication) because learners felt reluctant to claim mastery over skills they had only practiced briefly in a classroom setting.

During the Primo training, we collected the checklists and noticed an obvious pattern: about one-third of our learners marked "Need More Information/Training" for the objective "Request items from ARC [the library's on-site automated storage center] and other locations." This information let us quickly design a follow-up training focused exclusively on ARC requests. We also followed up individually with a few people who indicated a need for more training or information on some of the other objectives.

Evaluation Methods

If you're planning a relatively straightforward technical training, the outcomes checklist may be a good evaluation tool for you. Other types of training will lend themselves to different types of evaluation. I've listed a few below and offered some suggestions about where they will be most helpful. Remember that your evaluation should tie directly back to the stated learning objectives.

Testing:
A test can be oral or written, formal or informal. Use tests when your subject matter is factual/objective in nature and when you can provide right/wrong answers. Testing primarily measures *knowledge* objectives.

Observation:
Observation allows learners to demonstrate acquired skills. Use this method when your subject matter is technical- or process-oriented. Observation primarily measures *skills* objectives.

Debriefing/Discussion:
Talking with learners allows you to subjectively assess whether they "get it." Use this method when your subject matter is less factual/objective, more open-ended, or when testing and observation are not practical. Debriefing/discussion primarily measures *knowledge* and *attitude* objectives.

ACTIVITY

For each of your three learning objectives, identify at least one evaluation method you can use. Be specific about how you will evaluate; for example, if you want to evaluate by testing, what kind of test would you need to design?

Knowledge Objective:

_____

_____

_____

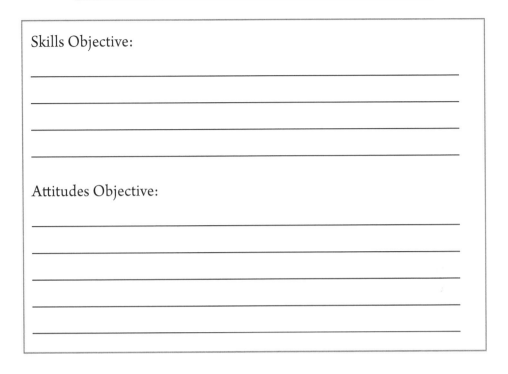

Skills Objective:

_____

_____

_____

_____

Attitudes Objective:

_____

_____

_____

_____

The Importance of Scope

When I began my training career, I worried a lot about how to pass on all of the knowledge I wanted my learners to gain, particularly when I was passionate about a subject. I think this is a typical tendency among more inexperienced trainers. Over the years, as I've coached and developed others, I've noticed that most people tend to start out overestimating how much content they can, and should, cover. This results in learners feeling overwhelmed with information and leaves little time for the kinds of engagement activities we'll cover in the next section.

As I've gained experience, I've learned to limit the scope of my training. Sometimes I learned this the hard way: by running out of time, by reading course evaluations that criticized my design choices, by noticing bored and restless body language. In general, learning to scope has been the product of refining my practice over a long period of time; after a while I developed an intuitive sense of what would and wouldn't work. Here are some of the questions I now ask myself when I'm designing.

What is the goal of this training?

The goal is not to turn everyone into an expert or even to pass on all of my knowledge. The goal is always to send learners away with something they can use. The objectives I used for the activity on pages 28 and 29 come from a real training session I presented. My goal was for learners to leave with an action plan for guiding a difficult conversation when they returned to work. I had to leave out a lot of great content about communication and conflict in order to keep the session focused on that.

What is the best use of our time in session?

Classroom time is always limited, sometimes more than I would like it to be. The difficult conversations session I presented was only 90 minutes long. The best use of time, then, was to allow learners to work through the template I had created. If I'd had three hours instead, I might have spent more time setting the stage with some introductory activities, facilitating open discussion about the topic, and having learners role play.

Am I trying to "write a book" here?

In the Introduction, I mentioned that I challenge myself with this kind of question all the time. When I'm intellectually engaged with the material, I start to think about all the great content I could present. But I have to remember that whatever I'm designing is meant to be a conversation, not a monologue: my training will occur in real, 3-D space, with other people present. I have to leave space for others to engage with the material. Otherwise, I may as well just write up what I want to say and distribute it without bringing people together.

ACTIVITY
Scope Your Training

What is the goal of your training?

_____

_____

_____

_____

_____

What is the best use of your time in session?

_____

_____

_____

_____

_____

How can you avoid "writing a book" and leave room for other people to engage with the material?

_____

_____

_____

_____

_____

_____

SECTION 3: DESIGNING FOR PURPOSEFUL ENGAGEMENT

Many years ago I had a chance to co-develop a four-day workshop focusing on organizational learning. It was intended to give people new insights and tools geared toward creating organizational structures that support continuous learning and improvement. My training partner and I presented this workshop repeatedly, which let us continually refine our design as we discovered what did and didn't work. The opening segment proved especially challenging; we wanted to kick off our event with an activity that would accomplish multiple goals:

- break the ice—let participants meet, mingle, and get to know a little bit about each other
- set the stage—introduce core themes and concepts that the rest of the workshop is built on
- start the cycle—get participants to reflect on past experience and connect it to the goals of the workshop

At the time, I was reading a lot about the creative process and had particularly been influenced by Robert Fritz's book *The Path of Least Resistance: Learning to Become a Creative Force in Your Own Life.* Our workshop was all about creating—we were trying to help people learn to create the kinds of organizations they wanted to be a part of. Fritz's book resonated with me because it emphasized creativity as a process that drives all kinds of human endeavors, not just the artistic ones that leap to mind when we hear the word "creative." I felt that if participants understood this, they would start to see themselves as people capable of creating new organizational realities.

I put this all together in an opening activity that illustrates what I mean by "purposeful engagement." Here's how it went:

1. I asked participants to think of something they had created—meaning, something they had brought into being. This could be work-related (a poster presentation for a conference, a new workflow process, a team, etc.) or more personal in nature (a garden, a family, a game, etc.).
2. I then instructed them to draw a representation of their creation using some markers and paper we provided.
3. Next, I asked everyone to stand up and hold their papers in front of them. On my cue, they were to begin circling around the room, looking at others' drawings. When they saw a drawing that intrigued them, they were to stop, introduce themselves to the other person, and spend a couple of minutes sharing information about their creations.
4. After about 10 minutes, during which time people had a chance to meet and talk to several other participants, I asked the group to take their seats again. Participants then introduced themselves to the whole group, including a short description of their creation.
5. After the introductions were completed, I asked the group to help me make a list of the factors that allowed them to produce their creations. What makes it possible for us to create something? What helps take us from an idea to a result? What pushes us toward the tangible products of our desires and goals? The list of factors usually included items such as "felt personally responsible": "something I really wanted"; "could envision the end product in my mind"; "had the right tools"; and "got help from others."
6. Referencing the list, I asked participants to relate this activity to the purpose of our workshop. What can our previous experiences with creating posters, workflows, gardens, games, etc. tell us about creating new models for the way our organizations work?

In total, this activity lasted no more than 30 minutes, and it accomplished all three of the goals I described above. I am sharing this example not because I think you should use it in your own training (30 minutes is not much time out of a four day workshop, but it's probably more time than you'd want to take out of a two hour training session). I am sharing it to stimulate your thinking about how to get learners actively engaged with the content and with each other.

Engagement means participants are taking responsibility for their own learning and contributing to the group. Engaged learners don't just passively receive knowledge, they construct knowledge. Engagement is not synonymous with activity (doing stuff) or entertainment (enjoying stuff). Learners are engaged when they are working through the learning cycle. Participants may be busy or having fun, but they may not be learning. Conversely, they may be learning without appearing to be busy or having fun.

Every activity in your design should clearly contribute to learning. You should be able to explain, if necessary, why you chose the activity and how it leads to learning outcomes. You should also be able to give participants clear oral or written directions that explain the purpose of the activity and/or describe the desired work product. The examples below show the difference between activities with an unclear purpose and those with a clear purpose.

UNCLEAR PURPOSE	CLEAR PURPOSE
Participants will discuss this idea at their tables.	Participants will relate the content to their own experiences by sharing real-life examples of this problem at their tables. Each table will share at least one example with the larger group.
We will make a list of factors that contribute to effective communication.	In order to define what we mean by "effective communication," we will describe specific behaviors and tools that we have seen effective communicators use. We will list these and refer back to them throughout the workshop.
We will watch a video.	We will watch a video demonstrating ineffective presentation skills. Participants will identify what the speaker is doing wrong and suggest what he could do to improve.

UNCLEAR PURPOSE	CLEAR PURPOSE
Participants will do a role play.	Participants will do a role play in order to see how the feedback model might work in a real conversation, identify the model's strengths and weaknesses, and practice the communication skills required to give feedback effectively.

Reflection Question

Reflection: *How could you clarify the purpose of each of the activities listed below? For each example, write a description that better explains the point of the activity.*

UNCLEAR PURPOSE	CLEAR PURPOSE
Participants will search for records in the catalog.	
Participants will see a demonstration of the new software.	
We will discuss how to apply this concept.	

Guided Engagement

My colleague and I thought very carefully about how best to engage learners in our Primo training. Technology trainings can have a tendency to become "show and tell"—with the best of intentions, a technology expert who doesn't understand training design can end up leading the group on a tour of a the product's features, without helping learners practice or understand how those features will benefit them in real life. Hands-on training sessions can be tricky when you have a roomful of people who have very different levels of ability and knowledge. Because of this, we wanted to make sure our Primo training was tightly designed, giving people maximum opportunity for engagement while keeping them focused.

The design we came up with, shown in the "Primo for Basic Users" handout in Appendix 4, blends self-direction (learners "doing" on their own) with guided instruction. I would call this approach "guided engagement." Each participant received a copy of the handout at the beginning of the session. We explained that we would use this handout as the structure for the training and asked everyone to stay with us—to avoid working ahead or getting distracted by other things on their screens. I've reproduced a small section of the handout here so that I can walk through each section and explain how it contributed to engagement.

Instructions gave learners a specific task that kept them focused on learning something related to our course objectives.

Questions prompted learners to find information on their own. This allowed people some autonomy and an opportunity to experiment with the new system. Solving specific "problems" let people familiarize themselves with the features and layout in an organic way. Because we were in a group setting, the questions also encouraged friendly competition and collaboration in finding the correct answers. The questions also served as an in-the-moment evaluation tool for us, because we could easily see which kinds of tasks were easy for people and which ones they struggled with.

Explanations allowed the trainer to point out details about the system's features and functions after learners shared their answers. As I mentioned earlier, this is the inverse of the approach I often see, where trainers introduce a feature/function and then (if the session is hands-on) encourage participants to try it out. Our approach allowed learners to have a little bit of self-acquired knowledge before we introduced a new concept. For instance, in Step 2, learners would have already noticed and used the "Refine My Results" sidebar on their own before we pointed it out to them. This meant that the information we gave them just expanded on something they were already a little familiar with.

Section from Primo Training Handout

STEP	INSTRUCTIONS	QUESTIONS	EXPLANATIONS
1.	Login to **My Library Account**		You'll need to be logged in to use some of the Primo features.
2.	**Search for** *Ute* and hit **GO**		We'll use these search results to walk through some of Primo's basic functions
		How many items in your search results are available in Special Collections? *Answer:*	The **Refine My Results** sidebar lets you find items according to specific criteria, which are called *facets* in Primo. The **Location** facet will tell you where the item is stored. You can also see the location in the brief item description on your **Results** list.

Once we had created the handout, we realized that we could use it for our more advanced learners as well—those who would be attending our "Primo for Patron Service" training. We knew that the best use of our in-session time with that group would be to cover the last four learning objectives (numbers 6-9) that you can see in Appendix 2. However, we couldn't just ignore objectives 1-5. We decided to distribute the handout in advance of the "Primo for Patron Service" training session, with the expectation that people in that group could (and would) work through it independently ahead of time. This ensured that everyone was familiar with the basic features but saved a lot of valuable instruction time.

Cohesive Structure & Flow

During the Primo training, the learning experience was held together by the way we sequenced our tasks (from simple to complex) and the way we connected them to each other. For example, the tasks in Steps 3-7 all built on the search results learners got in Step 2. How does a cohesive structure and flow enhance learner engagement? Consider your own experience as a television viewer. What is the difference between a variety show like *Saturday Night Live* and a sitcom like *Frasier*?

The variety show has a short-term goal: to make us laugh. It demands only that we pay attention for 2-5 minutes at a time. It throws a series of disconnected skits at us, hoping that a few of them will prove funny. Its characters are static (Wayne and Garth party on, and on), its situations are contrived (how does MacGruber survive repeated explosions?), and its takeaway value is superficial (what can we really learn from the Coneheads, besides how to consume mass quantities of beer and chips?).

The sitcom has both short- and long-term goals. It doesn't just try to hold our attention for a few minutes; it also wants the audience to be emotionally invested. It follows a narrative sequence to build suspense, resolve tensions, and develop relationships. Its characters are dynamic (consider how Frasier's relationship with his father, or Niles' relationship with Daphne, changed over the course of the show), its situations are relatable and grounded in reality (many Baby Boomers find themselves caring for an aging parent), and its takeaway value can be meaningful or even profound (how do I handle workplace/family conflicts? can I reinvent myself like Frasier does?).

Frasier offers a cohesive viewing experience that engages people fully and whose meaning extends beyond the moment. It uses **plot**, **character development**, and **theme** effectively. We can adapt and use these elements to enhance the effectiveness of training design.

> **Plot**: Sequence topics and activities deliberately and logically, to lead learners from one place to the next. Make sure that your design makes sense as a whole; each part should connect to what comes before and after. Your training should have a beginning (a short introduction to set the scene), a middle (where most of the action happens), and an end (a brief conclusion to wrap up loose ends).

> **Character Development**: Allow learners to grow. Build awareness and skills gradually. Start with simple or foundational ideas and activities and increase in complexity once learners have grasped the basics.

> **Theme**: Organize your training around a set of core ideas, concepts, and principles, and thread them throughout the session.

Deciding How to Deliver the Training

Entire books have been written about the different types of training methods you can choose from when it's time to decide how you're going to deliver your material. Appendix 5 summarizes the most commonly-used methods I'm aware of; it's not an exhaustive list, but it will give you plenty to work with. I recommend researching these methods more in-depth before using them for the first time or in potentially difficult/complex situations. Facilitating open discussion, for instance, requires a high level of preparation and skill when the subject matter is controversial/emotionally-charged. Games are a great way to inject a little excitement into your training, but you need to make sure you can pull people back to reality and the learning objectives afterward.

Below are some of the general criteria that will help you choose the right kinds of activities for engaging learners at different points in your training.

Alignment With Objectives

Knowledge-based objectives lend themselves to traditional instructional methods such as readings and lectures. Group discussions can be helpful if your goal is to generate (rather than deliver) information. Skills-based objectives require interactive methods that allow people to practice in a structured setting and receive feedback about their performance. For example, triads (groups of three) in a communication skills training allow participants to take turns in the role of speaker, listener, and observer and then discuss what each person did well/could improve on. Attitudinal objectives are best achieved when learners have an opportunity for an "aha" moment; individual reflection, group discussions, simulations, and games can provide these moments.

Sequential Development

The way you chain activities together influences the way learners develop. I mentioned earlier that in the Primo training, we decided to let people experiment with performing tasks before we gave them information about the system features and functions they were using. This sequence emphasized problem-solving over memorization of facts. When I want learners to internalize new ideas that may challenge existing ones, I usually begin with a discussion, reflection, or case study and then introduce whatever material I want to present. When I want people to learn how to use a particular approach to do something, I explain the approach first, then provide an example/demonstration, then give them a practice opportunity, and then follow up with a discussion about how the approach worked in practice versus in theory. There is no single right way to blend your activities, so don't agonize over this; just make sure you give some thought to how learners will acquire, process, and evaluate information.

Preparation for Application

The more learners will have to independently perform complex tasks back on the job, the more your activities should be geared toward deep engagement. When I conduct new employee orientations, I simply tell people information such as, "your proximity card gives you access to the staff entrance from 6 a.m.–6 p.m. on weekdays." I don't need to have them practice using their cards to open the door or pair off to discuss the access hours. I take a different approach for introducing the library's service standards. One of my librarian colleagues gives each new employee a handout describing the standards and asks them to quickly read through it. He then asks three simple questions that we spend the rest of that time exploring: "What does this mean to you? Does this make sense to you? Why are we doing this?" The combination of reading, reflection, and discussion makes it more likely that people will remember the standards when the time comes to actually use them. The next section of this book deals specifically with the issue of applying learning on the job.

SECTION 4:
DESIGNING FOR LEARNING TRANSFER

Several years ago I led a series of in-service trainings for the other members of my campus training department. During one session, I posed the following question:

> What makes a workshop worth the hypothetical $100 it costs for an employee to attend? Of these possible outcomes, which seem most valuable?

- enjoyed the session
- felt reenergized
- appreciated meeting colleagues
- thought the information would be helpful
- thought the material was relevant
- gained insight into a real situation on the job
- stopped doing something ineffective
- successfully applied a new idea, skill, etc. on the job

The point of this question was to emphasize that training's ultimate value depends on its **transfer**—the "degree to which trainees effectively apply the knowledge, skills, and attitudes gained in a training context to the job" (Baldwin & Ford).

Learning vs. Transfer

In Section 2, I explained how my colleague and I used the Training Outcomes Checklist to assess what people had learned in our Primo training. This checklist, however, only measured what people said they were able to do immediately after the training session. It didn't measure how successfully people performed when they returned to work. And in fact, a few weeks after our Primo implementation, we heard reports that some people were struggling. How could this happen if the vast majority of our learners marked "Can Perform/Understand" for most of the objectives?

Our training was focused on knowledge/skill acquisition—we were charged with helping people to understand and use certain features and functions of the new system. The checklists demonstrated that we accomplished that goal. But acquiring knowledge or skills in a classroom setting (learning) is a very different proposition than using them in a real setting (transfer). This is why, for instance, prospective pilots have to demonstrate flying proficiency to an instructor before they are allowed to solo.

Using any new skill reliably requires some trial-and-error that extends beyond an instructional session. People who have used the same online catalog for years will simply need time to become as proficient with a new one. Once we became aware of the difficulties some people were having, we were able to intervene to shorten the learning curve. We offered specialized training sessions to address the specific problems people had encountered. Our ILS administrators used our regular communication channels (email distribution lists and a daily "newsletter" type email that goes out to all employees) to raise awareness about the most common problems or questions they got from staff users and provide answers or troubleshooting advice.

Reflection Question

If you were in charge of the Primo training, what would you try to do to increase learning transfer?

_____

_____

_____

_____

Enabling Transfer

Transfer is influenced by the learner's characteristics (ability, personality, motivation) and the work environment (support and opportunity for use), but trainers have limited control over these factors. Trainers do have control over the third major factor influencing transfer: design.

How can you ensure that your training is designed for transfer as well as learning? Several years ago I conducted a literature review on transfer or training, specifically as it relates to applying complex skills on the job. The following design strategies will increase the chances of positive transfer.

Focus on generalizable principles. Learners appear to have a greater chance of transferring knowledge when they understand the purpose, assumptions, and systems behind specific skills and approaches. Principles that apply to many different situations serve as cornerstones on which to build skill sets.

Example: In the difficult conversations training, I described the "fight or flight" response and asked people to discuss how it might surface during such a conversation and how they could manage their own instinctive responses to conflict.

Relate principles and skills explicitly to the job. Learners need to see the correlation between what they experience in a classroom setting and what they experience in their own work environments. Practice opportunities should reflect as closely as possible the conditions, problems, and dilemmas learners face.

Example: When designing a university workshop on addressing performance problems, I asked my colleagues from Employee Relations to identify the most common responses employees have to corrective performance conversations. I then created role play/ simulation scenarios using those responses.

Practice skills in multiple contexts. Learners are more likely to reproduce classroom learning in real life when they have used new skills repeatedly and in a variety of situations. Practice opportunities should demonstrate how the same behaviors can transfer to diverse situations.

> **Example:** In the Primo training, we gave learners several different tasks that all required them to use the faceting feature, so that they would understand how to use this feature as a tool for narrowing down search results in many different ways.

Encourage learners to identify application opportunities. Learners need to recognize where new skills can help them and they need to prepare for using those skills in specific contexts. Trainers should provide learners with structured reflection and planning activities.

> **Example:** At the end of the organizational learning workshop, we asked participants to hold small group discussions centered on their takeaways—the concepts, principles, activities, etc. that most resonated with them. Following those discussions, we created dyads (groups of two) where participants shared their plans for applying what they had learned in their own organizations.

ACTIVITY

Which of these methods is best suited to your training?
What kinds of design strategies will you incorporate to
ensure transfer?

_____

_____

_____

_____

_____

_____

_____

_____

_____

_____

_____

_____

_____

_____

_____

_____

_____

_____

_____

_____

_____

_____

Identifying Application Opportunities

The last stage of Kolb's model, Active Testing, suggests that learning continues, and solidifies, when people leave a training session and begin using new ideas. I find it helpful to jump-start that process by explicitly preparing people for "re-entry" (going back to work with a new set of tools). This has the added benefit of reinforcing self-responsibility and personal accountability; people are more likely to follow through on applying what they have learned if they have committed themselves to doing so. Taking even a few minutes as you conclude your training to focus on application will ensure that everyone leaves with some notion of how to use what they have learned. Below are two examples I've used for different training sessions I have conducted in my library.

Training: Managing Relationships as a Supervisor
How can you use and build on what you've learned in this session? Take a few moments to capture the concepts, practices, and questions that stand out as important to you.

General Insights/Ideas to Think About

-
-
-

New Approaches, Skills, Tools to Try

-
-
-

Things to Learn More About

-
-
-

Training: Time Management
Commitment Worksheet
Date:

My Time Priorities This Week Are

-
-
-

I Plan to Achieve the Following Results This Week

-
-
-

I Will Do the Following to Stay Focused on My Priorities

-
-
-

I Will Be Accountable To:

-
-
-

ACTIVITY
Using the above examples as a model, create an application exercise/handout for your training.

CONCLUSION

I've often heard well-intentioned teachers and trainers claim that learning should be fun. I disagree. Fun is too low a bar to set for something as important as learning.

Journalists sometimes describe their role as one that comforts the afflicted, and afflicts the comfortable. I think teachers also play this dual role. Learning comforts us when we are afflicted by ignorance, doubt, and confusion. Learning brings us hope, confidence, and relief. Learning afflicts us when we are too comfortable in our routines, traditions, and beliefs. Learning brings us pain, uncertainty, and chagrin. And that's not a bad thing, if we work through it and use it to become better versions of ourselves. I hope, by reading this guide, you have discovered some tools that will make it easier for you to balance your dual role as helper and dis-comforter.

Appendix 1

MARRIOTT LIBRARY STAFF TRAINING COURSE DESCRIPTION

Course Name	Primo for Basic Users
Instructor(s)	Kate Holvoet
Date(s)	April 7, 2010
Audience	Staff who do not work at public service desks/on CITs

Type of Training (mark all that apply)

	Job-related
x	Organizational competency
	Professional/personal development
	Other:

Learning Objectives

This training will enable learners to:

1.	Identify the types of materials that are available through Primo
2.	Find books, journals, images, and digital objects in the basic search
3	Narrow search results using the "Refine My Results" sidebar
4.	Request items from the ARC and other locations
5.	Use the "My Library Account" and e-Shelf tools to review and save your searches

Post-Training Expectations (mark all that apply)

After the training, learners will be expected to:

	Perform new job functions
	Perform existing job functions with new software, equipment, processes, etc.
	Perform existing job functions with increased quality, efficiency, confidence, etc.
X	Meet organizational competencies related to this training
	Enhance effectiveness as an employee/professional
	Other:

Appendix 2

MARRIOTT LIBRARY STAFF TRAINING COURSE DESCRIPTION

Course Name	Primo for Patron Service
Instructor(s)	Kate Holvoet
Date(s)	2010
Audience	Staff who work at public service desks/on CITs

Type of Training (mark all that apply)

x	Job-related
x	Organizational competency
	Professional/personal development
	Other:

Learning Objectives

This training will enable learners to:

1.	Identify the types of materials that are available through Primo
2.	Find books, journals, images, and digital objects in the basic search
3	Narrow search results using the "Refine My Results" sidebar
4.	Request items from the ARC and other locations
5.	Use the "My Library Account" and e-Shelf tools to review and save your searches
6.	Understand how Primo pulls information from Aleph to create facets
7.	Perform an Advanced Search
8.	Guide patrons through using the new interface
9.	Follow the correct procedure for reporting catalog errors and problems

Post-Training Expectations (mark all that apply)

After the training, learners will be expected to:

	Perform new job functions
x	Perform existing job functions with new software, equipment, processes, etc.
	Perform existing job functions with increased quality, efficiency, confidence, etc.
x	Meet organizational competencies related to this training
	Enhance effectiveness as an employee/professional
	Other:

Appendix 3
MARRIOTT LIBRARY STAFF TRAINING OUTCOMES CHECKLIST

Course Name	Primo for Basic Users
Instructor(s)	Kate Holvoet
Date(s)	April 7, 2010
Learner	

		Can Perform/ Understand	Need More Training/ Information
LEARNING OBJECTIVES			
1.	Identify the types of materials that are available through Primo		
2.	Find books, journals, images, and digital objects in the basic search		
3.	Narrow search results using the "Refine My Results" sidebar		
4.	Request items from the ARC and other locations		
5.	Use the "My Library Account" and e-Shelf tools to review and save searches		

Appendix 4

PRIMO FOR BASIC USERS

Please follow the steps on this handout carefully. They are designed to lead you through the Primo interface in a structured, cohesive way. When you are finished, you should be able to:

☐	Identify the types of materials that are available through Primo
☐	Find books, journals, images, and digital objects in the basic search
☐	Narrow search results using the "Refine My Results" sidebar
☐	Request items from the ARC and other locations
☐	Use the "My Library Account" and e-Shelf tools to review and save your searches

To access Primo, copy and paste this link into your browser:
http://tinyurl.com/y9y2prm

STEP	INSTRUCTIONS	QUESTIONS	EXPLANATIONS
1.	Login to **My Library Account**		You'll need to be logged in to use some of the Primo features.
2.	**Search for** *Ute* and hit **GO**		We'll use these search results to walk through some of Primo's basic functions
		How many items in your search results are available in Special Collections? *Answer:*	The **Refine My Results** sidebar lets you find items according to specific criteria, which are called *facets* in Primo. The **Location** facet will tell you where the item is stored. You can also see the location in the brief item description on your **Results** list.

STEP	INSTRUCTIONS	QUESTIONS	EXPLANATIONS
3.	In your **Results** list, find the item titled, *A study of academic performance by Ute Indian children*	Where is this item located? *Answer:* If you wanted this item, how would you get it? *Answer:*	The **GetIt** link brings up a screen that will let you request an ARC item. This link will also let you request a Hold on an item (it will be pulled from the shelves and held at the Reserve desk). You must be signed in to your **Library Account** for this to work. This is one of the reasons we asked you to do that earlier. Signing in also lets you save information to your **e-Shelf**.
4.	Continue using these search results for the next two questions.	Without starting a new search, how would you find items dealing specifically with Ute Dwellings? *Answer:*	The **Subject** facet lets you narrow down your search to a more specific topic. If you didn't find Ute Dwellings listed, make sure you click "Show 14 more" to see all of the possible topics.
		How would you narrow down your search to only audio visual items (sound recordings, films, etc)? *Answer:*	The **Resource Type** facet lets you look for items in a specific format. You can also search for a specific format by using one of the drop-down menus just below the **Search for** box. The drop-down menus appear next to **Look for my query:**
5.	Find the drop-down menu with the "All items" default setting. Select "Audio Visual" from the menu and then hit **GO**		

STEP	INSTRUCTIONS	QUESTIONS	EXPLANATIONS
		One of the items on this **Results** list is titled *University of Utah Ute Marching Band*. How would you find more detailed information about this item? *Answer:* Can you find the name of the last song on the album? *Answer:*	The **Details** view gives you more information that might help you decide whether a particular item will meet your needs. If you are making a list of several items you want, you can use the **e-Shelf** to keep track of them. You can add items to your e-Shelf here, in the detailed record, or in the **Results** list like we did earlier.
6.	Add this item to your **e-Shelf**		We'll come back to the **e-Shelf** after doing one more search.
7.	The drop-down menu next to **Look for my query** is now set to "Audio Visual." It will stay that way until you reset it. Reset the drop-down menu to "All items." **Search for** *southern constellations* and hit **GO**		

STEP	INSTRUCTIONS	QUESTIONS	EXPLANATIONS
		What type of **Resource** is the first item on your **Results** list? *Answer:* What would you do if you wanted to see this item? *Answer:*	The **Image** icon on the left-hand side of the item listing tells you that this is an image. The **GetIt** link brings up a new window that allows you to see the image. This is the **item view** in CONTENTdm. This image is from our digital collections, which are now searchable in Primo.
8.	Close the CONTENTdm window. Look at your **Results** list again and add this item to your **e-Shelf**.		Now let's see what the **e-Shelf** can do for us.
9.	Click the **e-Shelf** button in the upper right corner of the screen.	How many items are in your **Basket**? *Answer:* How many different **Resource Types** are in your **Basket**? *Answer:* How many **queries** have you done during this **session**? *Answer:* What are the names of your **queries**? *Answer:*	The items in your **Basket** are the ones you have added to your **e-Shelf** during this **session**. A **session** lasts as long as you keep your browser open. If you are logged in, Primo will save your **Basket** from session-to-session. If you aren't logged in, your **Basket** will be emptied at the end of your **session**. Primo automatically saves your **queries** during a session. If you are logged in, you can **save** a **query** so you can go back and see the **Results** again later.

STEP	INSTRUCTIONS	QUESTIONS	EXPLANATIONS
10.	In the **Query name** list, click on the query named *southern constellations*.	How would you **Save** this query if you wanted to be able to come back and look at it tomorrow?	This shows you the **Results** you got when you originally searched for *southern constellations*. The **Save query** link on the left-hand side of the **Results** title bar brings up a new window that lets you give your query a new name and save it for later viewing.
11.	Click the **Save query** link. Enter a **Query name** of your choosing and press the **Save** button.		
12.	Return to your **e-Shelf**.	How many **Saved queries & alerts** do you have now? *Answer*: What is the **name** of your saved **query**? *Answer*:	

Appendix 5:
TRAINING DELIVERY STRATEGIES

Table 1: These are the basic levels of engagement you can use when seeking to make your training interactive. Each has advantages and disadvantages.

LEVEL OF ENGAGEMENT	ADVANTAGES	DISADVANTAGES
Individual Reflection Giving people private time to think/ write about a question or work on a problem/activity	Privacy = safety Encourages personal responsibility for learning Changes group energy	Can be difficult to slow down the group/maintain silence
Dyads/Triads Putting people into pairs/groups of three to practice a skill or work on a question, problem, activity, etc.	Allows more equal participation Provides safe space for learners to share/practice and give each other feedback	Information/ideas generated are not available to the whole group Some learners may not "click"
Small Group Discussion Breaking into subgroups to work on a question, problem, or activity; the trainer may divide up a set of questions, problems, information, etc	Allows learners to focus on a subset of information Gives learners more opportunity to exchange ideas and listen deeply	May surface problem group dynamics Sharing information with larger group (reporting out) can become tedious
Full Group Discussion Posing questions to the entire group and facilitating a focused but open conversation	Lets everyone hear the same information/ responses Can create shared understanding around common issues	May surface problem group dynamics Limits individual participation

Table 2: These are more specific and/or complex activities you might use to deliver content/engage learners.

METHOD/ ACTIVITY	BEST SUITED TO	PURPOSE	LIMITATIONS
Lecturette Giving a short lecture or presentation	Knowledge Objectives	introducing new concepts; delivering important information efficiently	Makes learners passive Can be dry/boring
Reading/ Watching Providing written or audiovisual materials for learners to read/ view	Knowledge/ Attitude Objectives	conveying complex information, esp. information with emotional content; analyzing ideas and situations	Limits interaction Can kill energy
Demonstration Showing the group how to perform a task	Skills Objectives	conveying performance goals/ standards; giving learners a frame of reference for practicing on their own	Doesn't take advantage of learners' experience or knowledge May be difficult to hold everyone's attention
Case Study Using a realistic scenario to illustrate a problem or concept and elicit responses about how to apply learning	Skills/Attitude Objectives	analyzing complex situations with multiple interdependencies/ "if-then" propositions	May seem too real or not real enough; learners focus too much on story details

METHOD/ ACTIVITY	BEST SUITED TO	PURPOSE	LIMITATIONS
Role Play Asking participants to pretend to take on specific characteristics or behaviors while responding to a fictional scenario	Skills/Attitude Objectives	modeling desired behaviors through positive examples; illustrating undesired behaviors through negative examples	Learners don't always stick with the role Requires explicit connections to real world applications
Simulation Asking participants to respond to a fictional scenario as themselves	Skills/Attitude Objectives	experimenting with using new ideas/ approaches in a low-risk setting; creating a "bridge" between classroom and real life	Some people will "role play" instead of being themselves Requires explicit connections to real world applications
Game Providing learners with a specific goal to achieve or task to be performed under a set of rules and constraints	Skills/Attitude Objectives	giving learners a real, in-the-moment experience where something is at stake; freeing imagination through play; eliciting cognitive and emotional responses	Can be time-consuming and logistically complex May seem frivolous Requires explicit connection to real-world application